Houghton
Mifflin
Harcourt

JOURNEYS
Close Reader

GRADE
2

Consumable

Printed in the U.S.A.

ISBN 978-0-544-86944-8

2 3 4 5 6 7 8 9 10   0029   25 24 23 22 21 20 19 18 17 16

4500628526   A B C D E F G

UNIT 1
Neighborhood Visit

UNIT 2
Nature Watch

UNIT 3
Tell Me About It!

UNIT 4
Heroes and Helpers

© Houghton Mifflin Harcourt Publishing Company • Image Credits: ©StokKete/Shutterstock.

UNIT 5
Changes, Changes Everywhere

UNIT 6
What a Surprise!

JOURNEYS

Close Reader

UNIT 1
Neighborhood Visit

Background Many cities around the world have zoos. A zoo is a place that keeps wild animals. People visit zoos to see the animals and to learn more about them.

Setting a Purpose Read to find out how some zoo animals are like other animals you might know.

All in the Family

by Katherine Mackin

①Read Underline the name of the zoo that this article tells about.

At the San Antonio Zoo, you can see many amazing animals. Some of these animals may have a family member living in your neighborhood!

② **Read** Circle the heading that tells what this section is about.

Different Kinds of Dogs

Bush dogs live in Central America and South America. They have straight, brown fur. In the wild, they eat large **rodents**.

Pet dogs come in all shapes and sizes. They may have floppy ears or curly hair. They eat food made for dogs. Pet dogs should wear collars.

rodents:

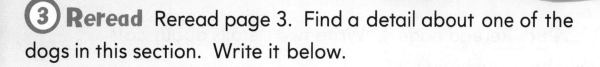

pet dog

③ **Reread** Reread page 3. Find a detail about one of the dogs in this section. Write it below.

_____

_____

_____

④ Read Underline the names of two types of cats in this section.

Cats of All Sizes

belong:

　　Lions **belong** to the cat family. They can grow up to eight feet long. Some have stood four feet tall. Lions hunt big animals in the wild.

　　Most house cats do not weigh more than fifteen pounds. They mostly eat special food for cats. However, some cats like to hunt for mice or birds.

house cat

⑤ Reread Reread page 4. Write two details about cats that tell about the heading.

_____

_____

_____

⑥ Read Circle the two headings on this page.

Large Lizards

Komodo dragons are the largest lizards. They can grow to ten feet long. Some have weighed five hundred pounds! The **saliva** of a Komodo dragon is dangerous. You would not want to be drooled on by a Komodo dragon!

saliva:

Little Lizards

Geckos belong to the lizard family. They are about eight inches long. Adult geckos weigh about one to two ounces. Geckos eat insects. They can eat ten crickets in a row.

gecko

SHORT RESPONSE

Cite Text Evidence Reread pages 2–5. What types of families is this article about? How do you know?

_____

_____

_____

Background People in a family often tell stories to each other. Sometimes grandparents tell stories about what life was like when they were children.

Setting a Purpose Read to find out about the stories a grandfather tells about a time long ago.

Grandpa's Stories

by Langston Hughes

① Read Read the poem. Circle two words that rhyme in the first four lines.

Grandpa's Stories

The pictures on the television
Do not make me dream as well
As the stories without pictures
Grandpa knows how to tell.

Even if he does not know
What makes a **Spaceman** go,
Grandpa says back in his time
Hamburgers only cost a dime,
Ice cream cones a nickel,
And a penny for a pickle.

spaceman:

SHORT RESPONSE

Cite Text Evidence   Reread the poem. What was life like back in Grandpa's time? Use details from the poem to explain.

_____

_____

Background Some people face special challenges such as not being able to walk or to see. Helper dogs can make life better for people with disabilities like this.

Setting a Purpose Read to find out how special dogs can help people with disabilities.

Helping Paws

① Read Underline a sentence that tells how dogs help people with disabilities.

Most people think of dogs as pets. For many people, dogs are family helpers! Some dogs help people who have disabilities. They give care to people who need it.

2 **Read** Circle the text that tells what to do when a guide dog is working.

guide:

Guide Dogs

Guide dogs help people who are blind or cannot see well. A guide dog learns sights, sounds, and smells of busy places. Guide dogs can go anywhere their owners need to go. They follow directions from their owners.

Guide Dogs Are Helpers

- Guide dogs help their owners walk safely.
- They follow directions to help their owners.

Make sure not to pet a dog when it is working.

3 **Reread** Reread the page. How does the photo help you understand what a guide dog does?

_____

_____

_____

④ Read Circle the caption on this page.

Hearing Ear Dogs

Hearing ear dogs help people who are deaf or who cannot hear well. These dogs listen for important sounds at home. An alarm clock and a doorbell are important sounds. When the dogs hear these sounds, they touch their owners with their noses. This gets their owners' attention.

Hearing ear dogs listen for the ring of a telephone or the sound of a smoke detector.

⑤ Reread Reread page 10. What are four things a hearing ear dog listens for? What does the dog do when it hears these things? Write the answer below.

_____

_____

_____

_____

© Houghton Mifflin Harcourt Publishing Company • Image Credits: ©Jim Corwin/Photographer's Choice/Getty Images

6 **Read** Underline the sentence that tells how hearing ear dogs help keep their owners safe outside.

When hearing ear dogs are outside with their owners, they listen for sounds that could mean **danger**. They help keep their owners safe.

danger:

Hearing Ear Dogs Are Helpers

- They listen for important sounds inside and outside.
- They let their owners know if there is danger.

SHORT RESPONSE

Cite Text Evidence Reread pages 8–11. In what ways do dogs help people who have disabilities stay safe? Write them below. Use examples from the text.

_____

_____

_____

_____

Background A swallow is a kind of bird. It likes to eat flies. A spider likes to eat flies, too.

Setting a Purpose Read this fable to find out a lesson that Spider learns about what she can do.

A Swallow and a Spider
A FABLE FROM AESOP

retold by Sheila Higginson

Cast of Characters

Narrator   Spider   **Swallow**

Narrator: A spider sat in her sticky web, waiting for dinner.

Spider: I hope some insects will stop by soon.

Narrator: Spider heard the buzz of flies floating in the breeze.

1 **Read** Circle the pictures of the two characters that this fable is about.

Swallow: Look at those juicy flies!

Narrator: Before the flies could reach her **web**, they were scooped up in Swallow's beak.

web:

Spider: Swallow is a pest! I will show him what I can do!

Narrator: Spider worked for a whole week. She spun a huge web.

Spider: Swallow doesn't scare me. I may be small, but I am dangerous, too!

Narrator: Spider put some berries in the middle of the web.

2 **Reread** Reread this page. Why does Spider say that Swallow is a pest? How do you know?

_____

_____

3 Read Underline the sentences that tell Spider's plan.

Spider: Swallow will smell these berries. Then he will get stuck in my net!

Narrator: Spider watched and waited, waited and watched.

Swallow: I smell something delicious. Those berries are just waiting for me!

Spider: Those berries aren't for you! Don't eat them! They are **rotten**.

rotten:

4 Reread Reread page 14. Does Spider want Swallow to fly into her web? How do you know? Write your answer below.

_____

_____

_____

14

⑤ Read Underline a sentence that tells what Spider learns about catching birds.

Narrator: Swallow scooped up the berries and flew right through spider's web! He didn't even hear spider screaming at him!

Spider: I can **judge** what I am good at doing. I am good at building webs to catch insects, but I am not a good bird-catcher. I'll go back to my web to wait for a juicy fly.

judge:

SHORT RESPONSE

Cite Text Evidence   Reread page 15. Why does Spider think she is not good at catching birds? Write your answer below.

_____

_____

_____

Background In the town of Westburg, a bus takes visitors on a tour. Visitors get to see all the interesting sights in the town. A map shows visitors where the tour goes.

Setting a Purpose Read to find out where the bus takes visitors in Westburg.

See Westburg by Bus!

1 Read Underline the sentence that tells where to get on Bus Number 33.

Welcome to Westburg!

The best way to see our town is on Bus Number 33. Get the bus in front of our Welcome Center. After you get on board, read this **pamphlet**. Just follow the numbers sprinkled on the map as you go. We are happy to share our wonderful town with you.

pamphlet:

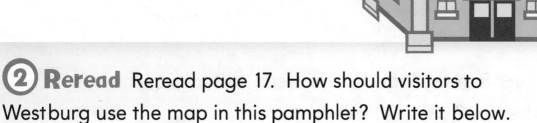

2 Reread Reread page 17. How should visitors to Westburg use the map in this pamphlet? Write it below.

_____

_____

③ Read On the map, circle the place where children can find computer games.

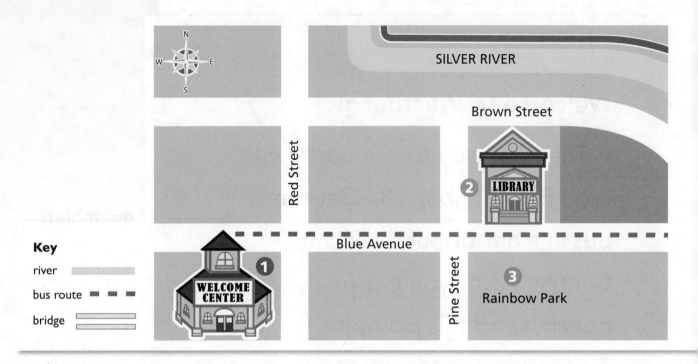

① Welcome Center

Find the Welcome Center. It is bursting with pamphlets, maps, and books about Westburg.

② Library

The Public Library is on Blue Avenue. The children's room is a great place for books, computer games, and movies.

③ Rainbow Park

Cross Blue Avenue to get to Westburg's largest park. People come here to play, walk, or have some quiet time.

④ Reread Reread page 18. How can visitors find the bus route on the map? Write it below.

_____

_____

_____

5 **Read** Circle a place on the map that is on Orange Street and White Avenue.

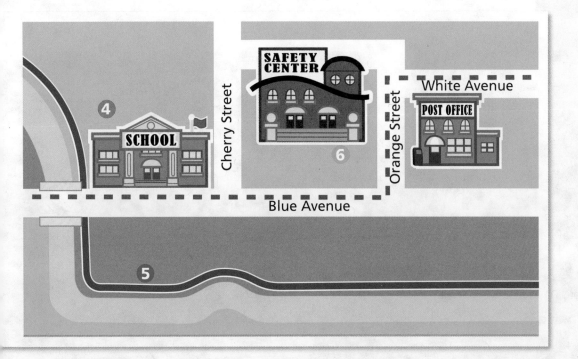

4 **School**

Take the bridge across the Silver River. When you get on the other side, Cherry Elementary will be on your left.

5 **Bike Path**

Have you noticed how the bike path follows the curves of the Silver River? What a great view!

6 **Safety Center**

If you suddenly hear siren noises as you pass the Safety Center, a fire truck or ambulance may be whizzing by!

SHORT RESPONSE

Cite Text Evidence Reread pages 17–19. Pick one place to visit. Use the map to tell where this place is.

_____

_____

_____

UNIT 2
Nature Watch

Background Some animals live in homes called nests. Other animals live in homes called hives. Some animals in the ocean live in shells. There are many kinds of animal homes.

Setting a Purpose Read to find out which animals live in these homes.

Whose Home Is This?

by Joli K. Stevens

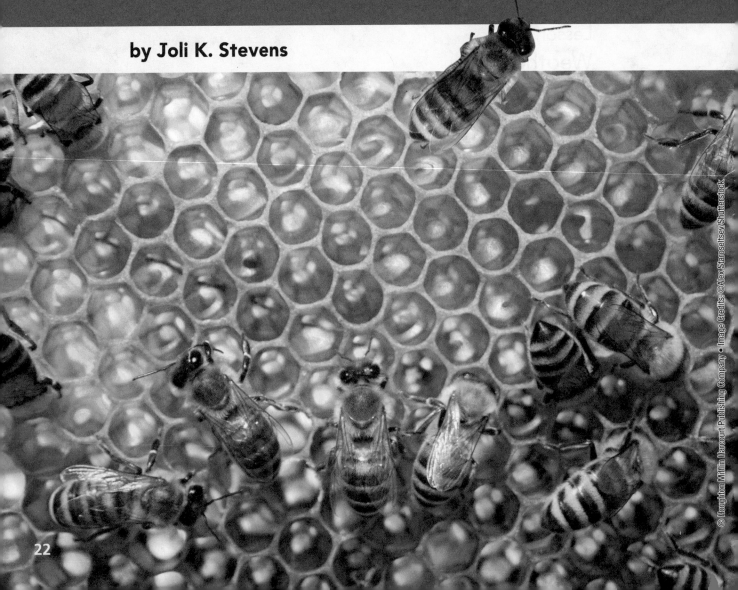

1 **Read** Underline a sentence that answers the question in the heading.

Why Do Animals Need Homes?

Animals need homes just like we do to stay safe and warm. Look at the pictures of animal homes on the next few pages. Can you guess what kind of animal might live in each home?

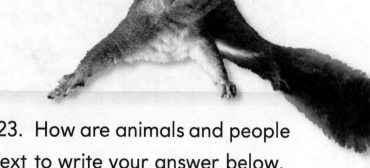

2 **Reread** Reread page 23. How are animals and people alike? Use details from the text to write your answer below.

_____

_____

3 Read Circle the heading that tells where this animal home is.

This Home Is Up High...

Many animals make their nests in trees. These nests are made from things the animals can find close by. Things such as leaves, twigs, **moss**, or feathers are used in nests.

Who lives here?

moss:

This nest looks like a pile of dead leaves and branches. It is an animal's home!

4 Reread Reread page 24. What detail lets you know why this home is up high? Write it below.

_____

_____

_____

24

⑤ Read Circle the text feature that tells who lives in this home.

Some squirrels live in trees.

Birds are not the only animals that live in tree nests. A large **cluster**, or bunch, of leaves and twigs high in a tree might be a squirrel's nest. Baby squirrels can stay in the nest for up to ten weeks. A squirrel might use a nest for a few months or even a few years. Sometimes squirrels will build more than one nest and use them all!

cluster:

Squirrels have large, strong claws that help them climb and jump.

⑥ Reread Reread page 25. How long might a squirrel use its home? Write it below.

_____

_____

⑦ Read Underline a sentence that tells more about the heading.

This Home Is Busy...

There are thousands of small insects that live and work together in this tree. This insect is often called busy because it is always working! Who lives here?

These insects are building their home.

⑧ Reread Reread page 26. Why is this home busy? Write it below.

_____

_____

_____

⑨ Read Underline the sentences that tell what kinds of work bees do in a hive.

Bees work together in a hive.

A beehive is made up of parts called combs. Bees make the combs out of wax from their own bodies. The **cells**, or small spaces, near the edge of the comb hold honey. The cells in the middle are where the queen bee lays the eggs. Some bees look after the hive. Other bees collect nectar from flowers to make their food, or honey.

cells:

A beehive is a very busy place.

⑩ Reread Reread page 27. What are two things that are in the cells in a beehive? Write them below.

_____

_____

_____

(11) Read Circle the heading that tells what this home can do.

This Home Can Move from Place to Place...

There are many kinds of animals that live in or near the ocean. Can you guess what kind of animal might live in a shell? Who lives here?

An empty shell like this one was once home for an animal.

(12) Reread What kind of home is this page telling about? Write it below.

_____

_____

13 **R**ead Underline a sentence that tells where this animal gets its shell home.

Hermit crabs carry their homes with them.

A hermit crab does not have a hard shell. It uses another animal's shell for cover. When an animal gives up its shell, a hermit crab may use it for its own. When a crab grows too large for its shell, it will **molt**, or cast off the old shell. Then it will get a new one. Would you like to live in a shell?

molt:

The hermit crabs along the shore can be very shy around people.

SHORT RESPONSE

Cite Text Evidence Reread pages 23–29. In what ways are a squirrel's home and bee's home different from a hermit crab's home? Write it below.

_____

_____

Background Pumpkins, beets, turnips, and cabbages are all vegetables. At some farms, these vegetables can grow very big. They can grow bigger than some children!

Setting a Purpose Read to find out how some farmers grow giant vegetables.

They Really Are GIANT!

by Judy Williams

① **Read** Underline a sentence that tells what "They Really Are GIANT!" means.

boring:

To some farmers, plain, ordinary-sized vegetables seem **boring**. These farmers think big. They like to grow the biggest vegetables ever.

CLOSE READ
Notes

© Houghton Mifflin Harcourt Publishing Company • Image Credits: ©Siegi/Shutterstock

30

② Read Circle the heading that tells what this section is about.

World Record Breakers

Plants are always blooming in California. The **scent** of rich soil fills the air. Every year in Half Moon Bay, the town holds the World Championship Pumpkin Weigh-Off. The judges all nodded yes when they saw the 2007 winner. It weighed 1,524 pounds, more than a big horse!

Pumpkins aren't the only giant veggies though. Some farmers use their muscles and heavy shovels to dig up 30-pound beets and turnips. Although these giants look tough, they are tender and delicious to eat.

scent:

③ Reread Reread page 31. What are three giant vegetables that grow in Half Moon Bay? Underline their names in the text.

④ Read Underline a sentence that tells where the "Home of the Giants" is.

Home of the Giants

Alaska might be the home of giant veggies. More giant vegetables seem to grow there than any other place in the world. Long summer days and good soil make veggies grow and grow. You can see 98-pound cabbages at the Alaska State Fair in Palmer.

Seven-year-old Brenna Dinkel from Wasilla, Alaska, looks small next to this giant wrinkled leaf cabbage!

⑤ Reread Reread page 32. What helps giant veggies grow in Alaska? Use details from the text to write a sentence that tells.

_____

_____

_____

6 **Read** Circle the part of the graph that shows how big a child is.

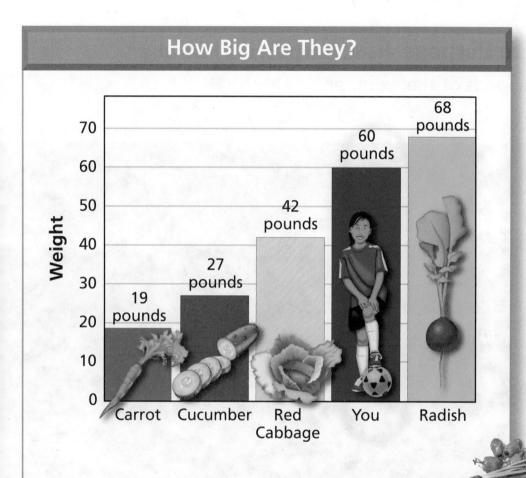

How Big Are They?

Weight

70
60
50
42 pounds
40
30
27 pounds
20
19 pounds
10
0

60 pounds

68 pounds

Carrot   Cucumber   Red Cabbage   You   Radish

SHORT RESPONSE

Cite Text Evidence Reread pages 30–33. How does the graph help you understand the rest of the text? Write your answer below.

Background Some poets write about the sights and sounds of the weather. Listen to the words that repeat in this poem. Do these words remind you of the sounds of the weather?

Setting a Purpose Read this poem to hear the different sounds of the weather.

Weather

by Eve Merriam

1 **Read** Circle some words and phrases that repeat.

Weather

Dot a dot dot   dot a dot dot
Spotting the **windowpane**.
Spack a spack speck   flick a flack fleck
Freckling the windowpane.

A spatter a scatter   a wet cat a clatter
A splatter a rumble outside.
Umbrella umbrella umbrella umbrella
Bumbershoot barrel of rain.

Slosh a galosh   slosh a galosh
Slither and slather and glide
A puddle a jump a puddle a jump
A puddle a jump puddle splosh
A juddle a pump aluddle a dump a
Puddmuddle jump in and slide!

windowpane:

SHORT RESPONSE

Cite Text Evidence Reread the poem. What details make the poem sound like rain falling? Write your answer below.

_____

_____

Background Real rabbits have short tails. This make-believe story tells why. Many stories like this give funny reasons for why things in nature happen.

Setting a Purpose Read to find out how Rabbit's tail helps him learn a lesson.

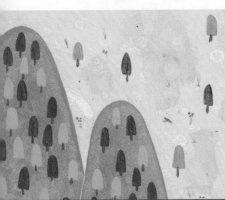

Why Rabbits Have Short Tails

adapted by Gina Sabella

CLOSE READ
Notes

① **Read** Underline two sentences that tell about Rabbit's tail.

curled:

Once Rabbit had a long, beautiful tail. It **curled** over his back like a furry fan. Rabbit was taking his family on a trip.

② **Read** Underline a sentence that shows what Rabbit thinks about himself.

"We have to travel in the direction of the stream," Rabbit said. "When we see the hill with the tallest height, we should head toward it."

When they spotted the tallest hill, Rabbit saw that they would have to swim across the stream.

Rabbit liked to **brag**. He told everyone how clever he was. He did not tell anyone that he could not swim. He did not want anyone to tease him.

brag:

③ **Reread** Reread page 37. Rabbit does not tell anyone he cannot swim. Write a sentence that tells why.

_____

_____

④ Read Underline the sentences that tell the animals Rabbit meets by the stream.

tunnel:

Rabbit saw a turtle crawling out of a **tunnel**. Ten tiny turtles followed behind.

"You have a large family," Rabbit said.

"Yes," Turtle replied. "My family is the biggest in the woods."

"I'm not sure," Rabbit answered. "My family might be bigger."

⑤ Reread Reread page 38. What does Rabbit do that shows he still likes to brag? Use details from the story to write the answer.

_____

_____

6 Read Underline the sentences that tell why Rabbit has a short tail.

"Line up your children across the stream," Rabbit said. "Then I can see who has a bigger family." Soon the turtles were lined up. Rabbit and his family jumped on their backs and skipped across the stream.

Turtle was not happy. He tried to grab Rabbit by the tail. But Rabbit's tail snapped off and he hopped away.

healed:

Even after it **healed**, Rabbit's tail never grew long and beautiful again.

SHORT RESPONSE

Cite Text Evidence   Reread pages 36–39. What lesson does Rabbit learn? Use details from the story to write the lesson below.

_____

_____

Background A photographer is a person who takes pictures called photographs. Many photographers like to take pictures of wildlife in the ocean.

Setting a Purpose Read to find out how some photographers take pictures under water.

Splash Photography

CLOSE READ
Notes

Smile!

How could you take a picture of a fish swimming under water? You would have to use special equipment, or tools.

People use underwater photography, or taking pictures, for different reasons.

scientist:
A **scientist** might want to learn more about sharks. Some people like it just because they think it is fun!

1 Read Underline three things that an underwater photographer wears.

Underwater Dress

To take pictures in deep water, a photographer uses a scuba tank, or air tank, to breathe. An underwater photographer also must take lessons to use a scuba tank.

An underwater photographer also wears a mask and swim fins. It is a good idea to wear a rubber suit called a wetsuit. These suits help to keep a person warm and safe from **stinging** animals.

stinging:

2 Reread Reread page 41. What does the photograph show you about what an underwater photographer does? Write the answer below.

_____

_____

_____

③ Read In the photograph, circle some wildlife that a photographer might take a picture of.

Using the Right Tools

camera:

An underwater photographer uses a special **camera** to take pictures. The camera is made to keep out water. There are other helpful tools, too. Some tools can be used to light up a dark place. Other tools help to get a closer look at a fish swimming by.

④ Reread Reread page 42. What are three types of tools that an underwater photographer uses? Write them below.

_____

_____

5 **Read** Look at the diagram. In the photograph, circle the scuba tank and the swim fins.

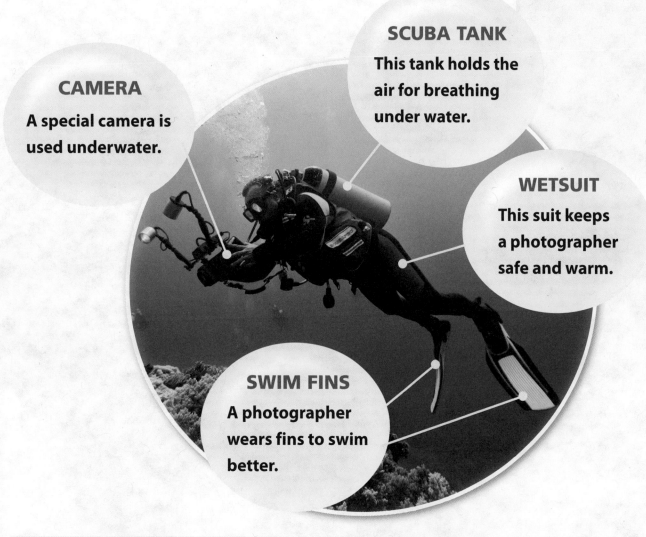

CAMERA

A special camera is used underwater.

SCUBA TANK

This tank holds the air for breathing under water.

WETSUIT

This suit keeps a photographer safe and warm.

SWIM FINS

A photographer wears fins to swim better.

SHORT RESPONSE

Cite Text Evidence Reread pages 40–43. What does the diagram on page 41 help you understand about the rest of the text?

_____

_____

_____

UNIT 3
Tell Me About It!

Background A sea lion is a large furry animal that lives near the ocean. Sea lions are great swimmers. A parrot is a bird. Many parrots are pets, like the one in this text.

Setting a Purpose Read to find out how two very smart animals can solve problems.

Talk About Smart Animals!

by Donald Logan

sea lion

1 **Read** Underline the names of the two animals in this text.

You may think only animals in storybooks or movies do things that seem **impossible**. You would be wrong!

Meet Rio and Alex. They are real-life animals. Rio is a sea lion. Alex is a parrot. These animals can do things that most people would never believe animals like them could do.

impossible:

2 **Reread** Reread page 47. What is special about Rio and Alex? Write a sentence that tells.

_____

_____

_____

3 Read Circle the heading on this page.

This Sea Lion Can Match

Rio is not like any other sea lion. She can solve a simple problem and tell the answer to her **trainers**! Rio has learned to look at three pictures and decide which two are most alike.

trainers:

Like the sea lions in the pictures on this page and page 49, Rio is a good swimmer.

4 Reread Reread page 48. How can this sea lion match? Write a sentence that tells.

_____

_____

_____

⑤ Read Underline a sentence that tells how Rio matches pictures.

First, Rio's trainers show her one picture. Rio studies it. Then her trainers add two more pictures. Rio points her nose at the picture that goes best with the first one she saw. When Rio is right, she gets a tasty treat.

Rio is not **impatient**. She takes her time before she answers.

impatient:

SHORT RESPONSE

Cite Text Evidence   Reread pages 47–49. Does Rio hurry when she has to match two pictures? How do you know? Write it below.

_____

_____

6 Read Circle the heading. Then underline the text that tells why Alex was not bad for a bird brain.

Not Bad for a Bird Brain!

Alex was an African grey parrot. Grey parrots in the wild are often seen gathered together in large groups. In the wild, parrots **communicate** using bird calls and other sounds. Alex was special because he had learned to talk. He knew over one hundred words!

communicate:

7 Reread Reread page 50. How was Alex different from parrots in the wild? Write it below.

_____

_____

_____

⑧ Read Underline a sentence that tells a problem Alex could solve.

Alex's owner had also taught Alex to tell colors apart and to count. Alex could even understand questions and answer them. Sometimes Alex would get tired. He would become **furious** and would demand a treat. After a break, he would go right back to solving problems.

furious:

SHORT RESPONSE

Cite Text Evidence Reread pages 47–51. In what ways do the headings help you understand the information in this text? Write it below.

_____

_____

_____

_____

Background Every song has a beat. The beat is the same sound over and over. People often tap their toes to follow the beat of a song.

Setting a Purpose Read to feel the beat in this song about the bottom of the sea.

There's a Hole at the Bottom of the Sea!

1 Read Underline a clue that tells what a *rhythm* is.

A song is like a poem that is set to music. A song has a rhythm, or a beat. Some songs also rhyme and have repeated words, just like some poems do.

Each section of a song is called a verse. The song you will read has four verses. Each verse has **repeated** words from the earlier verses.

repeated:

2 Reread Reread page 53. How is a song like a poem? Write it below.

_____

_____

③ **Read** Underline the lines in verse 1 that repeat three times.

1. There's a hole at the bottom
   of the sea,
   There's a hole at the bottom
   of the sea,
   There's a hole, there's a hole,
   There's a hole at the bottom
   of the sea.

④ **Reread** Reread page 54. How does the rhythm change? Write your answer below.

_____

_____

_____

54

⑤ Read Underline a phrase from verse 1 that repeats here.

2. There's a log in the hole
   at the bottom of the sea,
   There's a log in the hole
   at the bottom of the sea,
   There's a log, there's a log,
   There's a log in the hole
   at the bottom of the sea.

SHORT RESPONSE

Cite Text Evidence Reread pages 53–55. How does the song change in verse 2? Write it below.

_____

_____

_____

⑥ **Read** Underline a new detail that is added to verse 3.

bump:

3. There's a **bump** on the log in the hole at the bottom of the sea,
There's a bump on the log in the hole at the bottom of the sea,
There's a bump, there's a bump,
There's a bump on the log in the hole at the bottom of the sea.

⑦ **Reread** Reread page 56. What is happening to each verse as you keep reading? Write it below.

_____

_____

8 Read Underline a phrase from verse 1 that repeats here.

4. There's a frog on the bump
on the log in the hole
at the bottom of the sea,
There's a frog on the bump
on the log in the hole
at the bottom of the sea,
There's a frog, there's a
frog,
There's a frog on the bump
on the log in the hole
at the bottom of the sea.

SHORT RESPONSE

Cite Text Evidence   Reread the song. What makes the rhythm change from verse 1 to verse 4?

_____

_____

Background Pen pals get to know each other by writing letters or emails. The pen pals in this text live in different countries.

Setting a Purpose Read to find out what a student tells her pen pal about life at a school in America.

An American School

① Read Underline the names of the two pen pals.

Hi, my name is Lily. I go to Washington Elementary School. Aki is my pen pal from Japan. She came for a visit. She wants to ask me some questions about my school.

Lily

Aki

Aki: How did your school get its name?

Lily: My school is named after George Washington who was the first president of the United States. The president is the main leader of our country. The president **represents** our nation around the world. Our president lives and works in a special home called the White House in Washington, D.C.

represents:

_____

_____

_____

© Houghton Mifflin Harcourt Publishing Company

④ Read Underline the sentence that best answers Aki's question.

Aki: How do you start your day at school?

honor:

Lily: We start our day with a pledge to our flag. This is how we **honor**, or respect, our country and its people. Our flag is red, white, and blue and has stars and stripes. There are fifty stars, and each one stands for one of the fifty states in the United States.

⑤ Reread. Reread page 60. What do the stars on the flag of the United States stand for? Write it below.

_____

_____

6 Read Underline the subjects that Lily learns about in school.

Aki: What **subjects** do you learn about in school?

subjects:

Lily: We learn about math and science. We also read a lot of books and learn new words. My favorite subject is social studies.

SHORT RESPONSE

Cite Text Evidence   Reread pages 60–61. What is one thing that Aki learns about Lily's school in this interview? Write it below.

_____

_____

_____

_____

7 **Read** Circle the picture of the symbol of hope and freedom.

Aki: What are you learning about in social studies?

Lily: This week we are learning about **symbols** of the United States, like our flag. Our teacher said that the bald eagle is another symbol. It represents a strong and free country. The Statue of Liberty is also a symbol. When people see it, they think of hope and freedom.

symbols:

8 **Reread** Reread page 62. What does a bald eagle represent to people in the United States? Write it below.

_____

_____

⑨ Read Underline the reason that Lily likes music class.

Aki: What are some fun things you do at school?

Lily: I like our music class because we get to sing our favorite songs and play **musical instruments**. This week we played drums and bells. I also like going to check out books at our school library!

musical instruments:

SHORT RESPONSE

Cite Text Evidence   Reread pages 58–63. What are some things that Aki learns from Lily by asking her questions? Write them below.

_____

_____

_____

_____

Background Braille is a type of writing made by little bumps on a page. The bumps stand for letters and words. People who cannot see can touch the bumps. They can read the words with their fingers.

Setting a Purpose Read to find out how special tools help people who cannot see.

Talking Tools

①Read Underline a sentence that tells why people who cannot see use Braille.

knowledge:

Helen Keller lived in darkness, but she was curious about the world. Braille helped Keller gain **knowledge**. Today people who cannot see still use Braille to help them read.

2 Read Circle the ATM in the photograph.

Many ATMs (Automated Teller Machines) have Braille labels, for example. That way, blind people can use them to do their **banking**. Some ATMs even talk! With just one quick motion, users plug headphones into the ATM. Then the ATM tells them what to do.

banking:

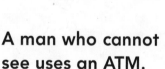

A man who cannot see uses an ATM.

3 Reread Reread page 65. How can blind people use their ears to do their banking? Write it below.

_____

_____

_____

④ **Read** Underline a sentence that tells how people read their notes on the notepad.

computer:

A Braille notetaker is a **computer** that helps people who cannot see. They type their notes on it, using a Braille keyboard. The notes are saved in Braille. Later they can use their fingers to read the notes in silence on the notepad. The machine can also read the notes aloud!

SHORT RESPONSE

Cite Text Evidence Reread pages 64–66. How are many ATMs and the Braille notetaker alike? Use details from the text to write your answer below.

_____

_____

_____

⑤ Read Circle the dot keys in the diagram of the Braille notetaker.

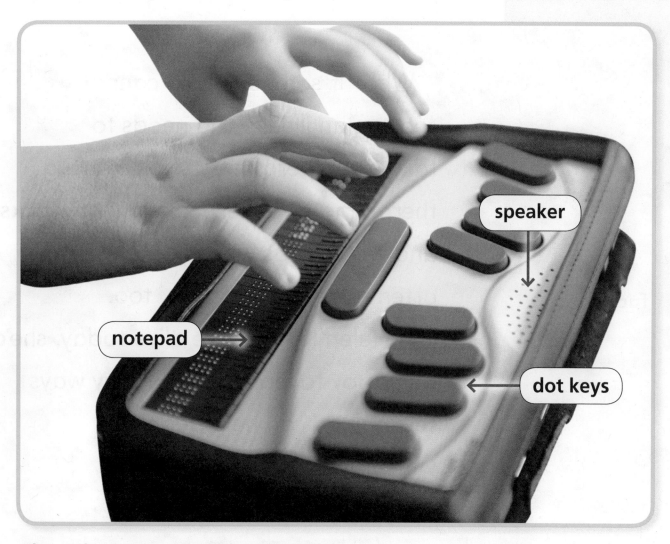

This girl is using a Braille notetaker. It uses an imitated human voice to read aloud.

⑥ Reread Reread the caption and look at the diagram. What part of the notetaker does the imitated human voice come from? Write it below.

_____

_____

7 **Read** Underline the names of three devices that help people with vision disabilities.

What if someone who cannot see has an illness and needs to take a temperature? Use a talking thermometer! There are talking clocks and watches as well. These watches often have Braille **faces**, too.

faces:

If Helen Keller were alive today, she'd be happy to learn of the many ways technology can help people with vision disabilities.

8 **Reread** Reread page 68. Why might someone use a talking thermometer? Use details from the text to write the answer below.

_____

_____

© Houghton Mifflin Harcourt Publishing Company

⑨ Read Circle the part of the diagram that shows how to change the volume.

Braille labels

Button to increase volume

Some phones have large numbers and Braille labels. Otherwise, their behavior is just like that of any other phone.

SHORT RESPONSE

Cite Text Evidence Reread pages 64–69. What might Helen Keller use to do her banking and to take notes if she were alive today? Use examples from the text. Write them below.

_____

_____

Background Fire is very dangerous. So people need to follow safety rules. These rules keep people safe during a fire.

Setting a Purpose Read to find out what two children tell their father about fire safety at home.

Readers' Theater

Safety at Home

by Margaret Sweeny

Cast of Characters

- Dad
- Alexa
- Jake

1 **Read** Underline the dialogue that shows Dad wants to know about the children's class trip.

Dad: What did you do on your class trip?

Alexa: We visited an **enormous** fire station.

enormous:

Jake: The fire chief gave a speech about fire safety.

Dad: I hope you were paying attention.

Alexa: We were. Later, we worked with a buddy to make a safety poster. I worked with Jake.

2 **Reread** Reread page 71. Who are the characters that speak dialogue here? Write them below.

_____

_____

3 **Read** Underline what Alexa says about get low and go.

Jake: Look at our poster.

Dad: I'm shocked! You know more about fire safety than I do.

obeys:

Alexa: Everyone in our school **obeys** fire safety rules.

Jake: Guess what <u>get low and go</u> means?

Alexa: If the house is smoky, get low.

STOP, DROP, AND ROLL
1. If your clothes catch on fire, don't run.
2. STOP where you are.
3. DROP to the ground. Cover your face with your hands.
4. ROLL over and over to put out the fire.

4 **Reread** Reread page 72. Which character tells about what everyone does at the children's school? Write it below.

_____

_____

5 Read Underline the dialogue that shows what Dad wants the family to do.

Jake: That's because smoke **rises.** Get low to stay below the smoke.

rises:

Alexa: Crawl to the nearest way out.

Jake: Then go to a safe meeting place to wait for your family.

Dad: Let's pick a meeting place right now!

SHORT RESPONSE

Cite Text Evidence Reread pages 71–73. What do Alexa and Jake know about fire safety? How do you know? Write it below.

UNIT 4
Heroes and Helpers

Background Many schools have clubs children can join. A club is a group of people who join together because they are interested in the same things.

Setting a Purpose Read to find out ways the Helping Hands Club helps people.

The Jefferson Daily News

November 5

① **Read** Underline the headline that tells what this article is about.

Club Helps in Many Ways

by Ben Watts

The Helping Hands Club is one of the best clubs at Jefferson Elementary School. The children in this club volunteer their time to help other people and the community.

2 **Read** Circle the text that tells what the photograph shows.

Last month they gathered items to recycle from home and school. Many items, such as water bottles and juice containers, were placed in recycle bins. Some other items were used in the art classroom.

The club's sponsor, Mrs. Waters, was proud of all who helped. "Students created beautiful artwork from cloth and paper scraps. The club's hard work gave these items a new purpose," she said.

Art made from scraps

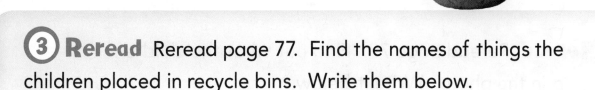

3 **Reread** Reread page 77. Find the names of things the children placed in recycle bins. Write them below.

_____

_____

④ **Read** Circle the name of the thing that the bake sale will help.

The Helping Hands Club has done many more things to help the community. They cleaned up the park and playground and collected food for the food bank. They had a bake sale to raise money for the animal shelter. Club members even decorated posters for bike safety week.

Malik is one of the members of the club. He told how the club helped someone he knew. "The Helping Hands Club helped my neighbor, Mrs. Dodge," he said. "She is 80 years old and lives alone.

The club helps to clean up the park.

⑤ **Reread** Reread page 78. Find out what the children are doing in the photo. Write it below.

_____

_____

6 Read Underline the sentences that tell what children can do at the meeting.

Our parents brought her hot food, and we pulled weeds in her yard. She was so happy and thankful, and she gave us all lemonade. Helping her made me feel happy, too!"

The Helping Hands Club would like to invite you to a meeting. You can find out what the club is all about and how you can **participate**. You can even share your own ideas! "This club helps in many ways," said Principal Ramirez. "It is a great club to join!"

participate:

SHORT RESPONSE

Cite Text Evidence Reread pages 76–79. In what ways did the club help the community? Write them below.

_____

_____

_____

Background Major League Baseball is made up of the top baseball teams in the world. Long ago, African Americans were not allowed to play on those teams. Jackie Robinson changed that.

Setting a Purpose Read to find out how Jackie Robinson became the first African American in Major League Baseball.

Jackie Robinson

1 **Read** Circle the text on this page that tells you what the photograph shows.

Young Jackie

Jackie Roosevelt Robinson was born on January 31, 1919, in Cairo, Georgia. He and his family soon moved to Pasadena, California. Jackie was good at sports, even as a young boy. He loved to run, play, and have fun with his friends.

Jackie was the youngest child in a family of athletes.

2 **Reread** Reread page 81. What does this part of the text tell about Jackie Robinson? Write it below.

_____

_____

Jackie Grows Up

In high school and college, Jackie didn't sit on the **curb** and watch others play sports. He would practice a lot. Jackie was good at football, baseball, basketball, and track. Fans cheered for him when he played.

curb:

Into the Major League

In 1947, Jackie became the first African American to play Major League Baseball. Before that time, African Americans were not allowed to play in the major leagues.

Jackie was famous for stealing bases. In this photo, he hurried to get to home plate.

④ **Reread** Reread page 82. What does the photograph show about Jackie Robinson? Write it below.

_____

_____

© Houghton Mifflin Harcourt Publishing Company • Image Credits: ©Bettmann/Getty Images

5 Read Circle the name of the section that tells what Jackie did after he stopped playing.

retires:

Jackie played for the Brooklyn Dodgers. The position he played was second base. Fans would stay to watch him if a game went into extra innings. They roared when the team won.

Jackie Retires

Jackie played his final game on September 30, 1956. After that, he worked hard to change laws that were unfair to African Americans.

In 2001, every Major League Baseball team honored Jackie. Every player wore Jackie's number 42.

SHORT RESPONSE

Cite Text Evidence   Reread pages 82–83. Why was Jackie Robinson important in America? How do you know? Write it below.

_____

_____

_____

Background A period is a tiny round dot in a sentence. It lets you know that you have reached the end of the sentence. What would a period do if it could roll away like a ball?

Setting a Purpose Read this poem about a period and listen for the rhythm in the words.

The Period

by Richard Armour

① Read Read the poem. Circle the two words that rhyme at the end.

The Period

Fat little period, round as a ball,
You'd think it would roll,
But it doesn't
At all.
Where it stops,
There it plops,
There it stubbornly stays,
At the end of a sentence
For days and days.

budge:

"Get out of my way!"
Cries the sentence. "Beware!"
But the period seems not to hear or to care.
Like a stone in the road,
It won't **budge**, it won't bend.
If it spoke, it would say to a sentence,
"The end."

SHORT RESPONSE

Cite Text Evidence Reread the poem. What words give you the idea that the period could roll away?

_____

_____

_____

Background Signs tell people where to go. They tell people in cars when to stop. They also tell where people can get food or a place to rest.

Setting a Purpose Read this play to find out how people in a car try to follow signs on a road.

The Trouble with Signs

by Bebe Jaffe

Cast of Characters

Ana

Ben

Fresh Berries
Turn left at the fork.

Polly's Place

1 **Read** Underline the words that tell what Ben is doing.

Ben: (steering a car) I'm glad we agreed to drive to the town meeting. We can look at the scenery.

Ana: (reading the pretend sign) Fresh berries. Turn left at the **fork**. Yum!

Ben: Where's the fork?

Ana: Do we need a fork to eat the berries?

Ben: I'm talking about a fork in the road!

Ana: I get it! You've got SO much wisdom, Ben.

2 **Reread** Reread page 87. What type of fork does Ana think they need at first? How do you know? Write it below.

_____

_____

③ Read Underline the dialogue about why people might go to Polly's Place.

Ben: I hope you are being polite and not teasing me.

Ana: (reading another sign) Do you have car trouble? Come to Polly's Place for some R and R. What's R and R?

relaxation:

Ben: R and R stands for Rest and **Relaxation**.

Ana: I'm glad that's cleared up, but do cars go to a special place for R and R?

Ben: (shaking his head) No, Ana. PEOPLE do.

④ Reread Reread page 88. What does R and R stand for? Write it below.

_____

_____

⑤ Read Underline the dialogue that shows Ben is frustrated with Ana.

Ana: Right! Listen to this sign! Have you failed in the kitchen? Are you tearing out your hair? Come to Carla's Cooking Class. Ouch! Do people tear their hair out because they overcooked a roast?

Ben: (losing patience) NO, Ana! That's just a saying. It means someone is getting **frustrated**.

Ana: Pull in! This is our meeting place.

Ben: Just in time! I'm tired of being your assistant.

frustrated:

SHORT RESPONSE

Cite Text Evidence Reread pages 87–89. How do you know Ana does not know what all the signs mean? Write it below.

_____

_____

Heroes Then and Now

①Read Underline a sentence that tells what a hero does.

What makes a hero? A hero does something brave or works hard to help others. A hero doesn't give up when things are hard.

Heroes come from different backgrounds and different places. They can be young or old. All heroes are important people, whether they lived in the past or do good **deeds** today.

deeds:

②Reread Reread page 91. What does a hero do when things are hard? Write it below.

_____

_____

③ **Read** Circle the names of the two heroes in the chart.

pilot:

THEN	NOW
These heroes reached for the stars.	
Amelia Earhart	**Ellen Ochoa**
Amelia Earhart became the first woman **pilot** to fly across the Atlantic Ocean.	Ellen Ochoa became the first Hispanic woman to travel in space.
Amelia studied hard before flying. She spent time with other pilots, gazing at maps and weather charts.	Exercise is important to prepare for space flights. Ellen exercises until her muscles are sore.

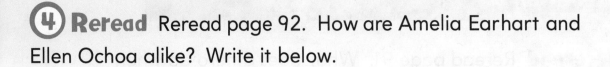

④ **Reread** Reread page 92. How are Amelia Earhart and Ellen Ochoa alike? Write it below.

_____

_____

_____

5 **Read** Circle the part of the chart that tells how Sacagawea and Earl Morse are alike.

THEN	NOW
The heroes in this chart helped others.	
Sacagawea	**Earl Morse**
Sacagawea was a Native American woman who lived over 200 years ago. She helped a group of early American explorers.	Earl Morse had an idea to honor veterans. Veterans are men and women who have been in the military. Some veterans were in the military during times of war.
Sacagawea helped the **explorers** find food and learn about the land. She helped them talk to Native Americans that they met.	Morse helped to start a group that helps pay for veterans to travel to Washington, D. C. There the veterans can see memorials and monuments that honor them.

explorers:

SHORT RESPONSE

Cite Text Evidence   Reread pages 92–93. How is the information in the two charts alike and different? Write it below.

_____

_____

_____

UNIT 5
Changes, Changes Everywhere

Background The equator is an imaginary line around the middle of Earth. Places near the equator are mostly hot. Places far from the equator are mostly cold.

Setting a Purpose Read to find out about one type of penguin that lives far from the equator.

Emperor Penguins

① Read Circle the part of the electronic menu that tells what this page is about.

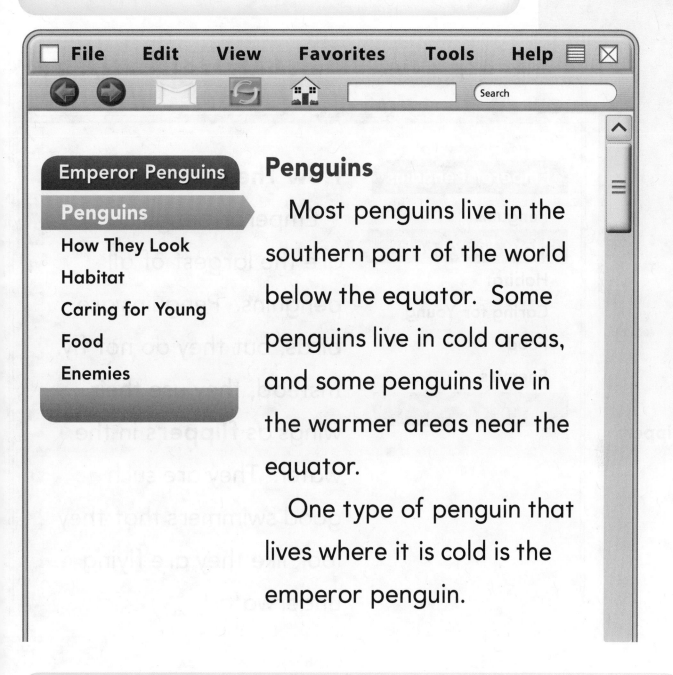

File   Edit   View   Favorites   Tools   Help

Search

Emperor Penguins

Penguins

How They Look

Habitat

Caring for Young

Food

Enemies

Penguins

Most penguins live in the southern part of the world below the equator. Some penguins live in cold areas, and some penguins live in the warmer areas near the equator.

One type of penguin that lives where it is cold is the emperor penguin.

② Reread Reread page 97. What does this website page tell about all penguins? Write it below.

_____

_____

_____

③ Read Circle the part of the electronic menu that might tell what these birds eat.

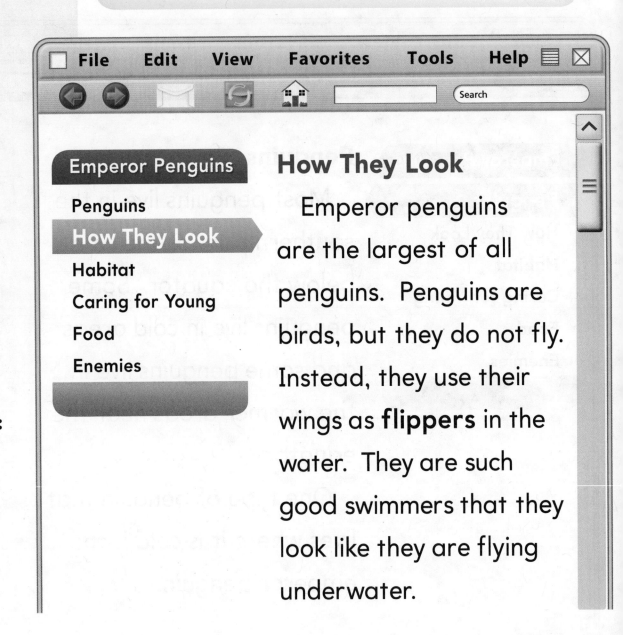

| File | Edit | View | Favorites | Tools | Help |

Search

Emperor Penguins

Penguins

How They Look

Habitat

Caring for Young

Food

Enemies

flipper:

How They Look

Emperor penguins are the largest of all penguins. Penguins are birds, but they do not fly. Instead, they use their wings as **flippers** in the water. They are such good swimmers that they look like they are flying underwater.

④ Reread Reread page 98. What do emperor penguins look like when they are swimming? Write it below.

_____

_____

5 Read Circle an icon you would click on to see more photos of emperor penguins.

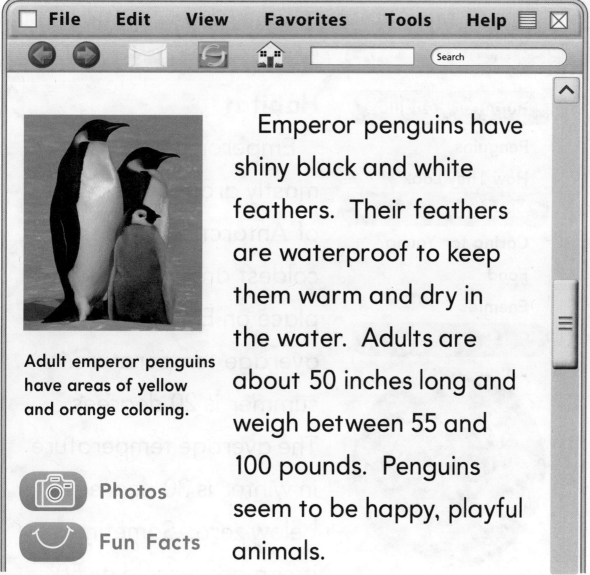

Adult emperor penguins have areas of yellow and orange coloring.

Photos

Fun Facts

Emperor penguins have shiny black and white feathers. Their feathers are waterproof to keep them warm and dry in the water. Adults are about 50 inches long and weigh between 55 and 100 pounds. Penguins seem to be happy, playful animals.

SHORT RESPONSE

Cite Text Evidence   How do an emperor penguin's feathers help it? Use details from the website to write it below.

_____

_____

6 Read Circle two places on this page that name this section of the article.

habitat:

Antarctica is located at the South Pole.

File　　Edit　　View　　Favorites　　Tools　　Help

Search

Emperor Penguins

Penguins
How They Look
Habitat
Caring for Young
Food
Enemies

Habitat

Emperor penguins live mostly around the coast of Antarctica. It is the coldest and windiest place on Earth. The average temperature in summer is 20 degrees.

The average temperature in winter is 30 degrees below zero. Sometimes it can get as cold as 50 degrees below zero!

7 Reread Reread page 100. How do you know emperor penguins can live in cold weather? Write it below.

_____

_____

8 Read Circle an icon that you would click on to read fun facts about emperor penguins.

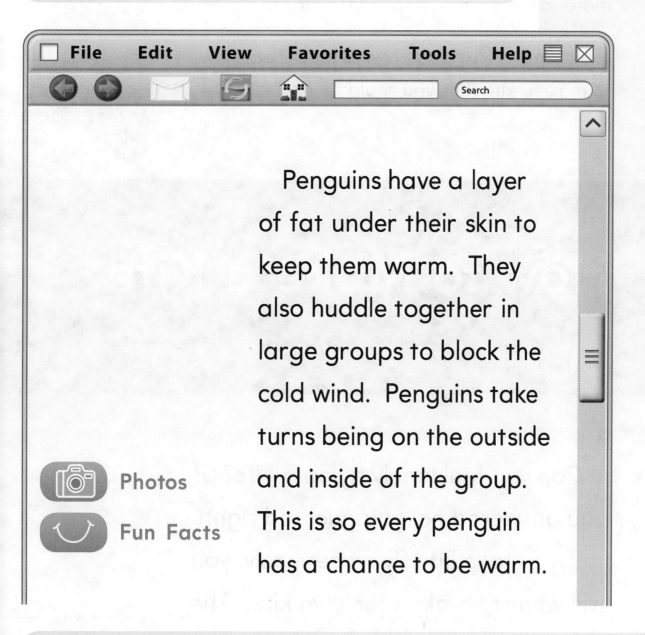

| File | Edit | View | Favorites | Tools | Help |

Search

Penguins have a layer of fat under their skin to keep them warm. They also huddle together in large groups to block the cold wind. Penguins take turns being on the outside and inside of the group. This is so every penguin has a chance to be warm.

Photos

Fun Facts

SHORT RESPONSE

Cite Text Evidence   Reread pages 100–101. What does this part of the website tell about emperor penguins? Write it below.

_____

_____

_____

Background Many people like to fly kites. Some people make their own kites. They make them with materials like sticks, paper, and string.

Setting a Purpose Read to find out how to make a kite that you could fly.

How to Make a Kite

by Joanna Korba

Can you feel lonely flying a kite? If you answered no, you guessed right!

If you take kite flying seriously, you will want to make your own kite. The first step in planning your kite is to read all of these directions. You may want to copy them onto another sheet of paper first.

1 Read Circle the things you need to make a kite.

Materials

2 sticks with small
cuts on both ends

24 inches

18 inches

5 pieces of ribbon

string

colored
paper

glue and
scissors

What to Do

1 First, make a **cross** with the sticks. Tie a string around the middle.

cross:

2 Reread Reread page 103. What is the first thing you do to make a kite? Write it below.

_____

_____

③ Read What do you do after you make the kite frame? Circle the picture that shows that step.

2 Run string around the edge to make a frame. Tie it tightly at the top end. Then cut the string.

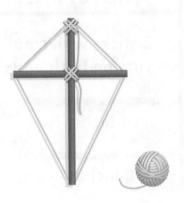

3 Lay the kite frame on the paper. Cut the paper so that it is slightly larger than the kite frame.

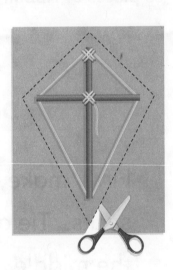

④ Reread Reread page 104. How do the pictures help you follow the directions? Write a sentence that tells.

_____

_____

5 **Read** Underline what will happen with too many ribbons.

4 Fold the paper over the kite frame. Glue it down. Then tie a long string to the middle of the frame.

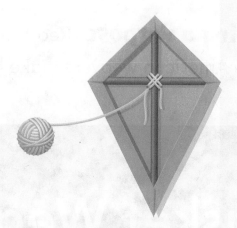

5 Cut a piece of string 36 inches long and make the tail. Tie a ribbon to the string every 6 inches with a tight knot. Too many ribbons will make your kite fly **heavily**.

heavily:

SHORT RESPONSE

Cite Text Evidence   What are the last two steps for making a kite? Write them in your own words below.

_____

_____

Background Baskets are made by weaving. A weaver uses long, thin pieces of grass and other materials. Some weavers use the long twigs from willow trees to make baskets.

Setting a Purpose Read to find out how some Native American weavers make baskets.

Basket Weaving

by Becky Manfredini

1 **Read** Underline three sentences that tell what baskets are used for.

A Native American Tradition

Some Native Americans weave beautiful baskets in many shapes and sizes. Some are for **storing** delicious foods. Others are to store clothes in. Some baskets are even used for carrying water! Basket makers make baskets for themselves and to sell.

storing:

2 **Reread** Reread page 107. Why do basket makers make baskets? Write it below.

_____

_____

107

③ Read Underline two types of materials that basket makers use.

Gathering Materials

Rug weavers have to make the material they use to weave rugs by spinning wool into yarn. Basket makers use **strands** of willow or special grasses to weave their baskets. After sharpening their cutting tools, basket makers go to places where the materials grow and cut off as much as they need.

strands:

Weaving is a tradition. Mothers teach their daughters how to weave.

④ Reread Reread page 108. What is the first thing basket makers do before they cut strands of willow or grass? Write it below.

_____

_____

⑤ Read Underline the text that tells why basket makers soak willow strands in water.

How to Weave a Basket

Basket makers prepare the willow strands by soaking them in water. That makes them soft and easy to bend. It makes the strands much easier to weave. Then they weave the strands into a pattern. Basket makers use dye they make from plants to make their baskets colorful. No basket is just like any other basket. The patterns are never **duplicated**. It takes a lot of skill to weave a beautiful basket.

duplicated:

The weaver holds thin strips of willow tightly as she works on this type of basket.

SHORT RESPONSE

Cite Text Evidence   Reread pages 107–109. What steps do Native American basket makers follow to make baskets?

_____

_____

_____

Background A lion is a big, strong cat that roars. A mouse is a tiny creature that runs along the ground. How can a tiny mouse help a big lion?

Setting a Purpose Read to find out what happens when a mouse finds a lion in trouble.

The Lion and the Mouse

1 **Read** Underline the detail that tells why the lion woke up.

Once a lion was sleeping peacefully in the grass. Then a mouse ran up his tail. The lion woke up. He grabbed the mouse and **flung** it. The mouse went tumbling across the ground.

"Please don't eat me," the mouse cried. "I promise that I will help you one day if you let me go."

flung:

2 **Reread** Reread page 111. What does the mouse tell the lion the mouse will do one day? Write it below.

_____

_____

③ Read Underline two sentences that tell how the lion knows that hunters must be near.

"You help me?" the lion laughed. "I will let you go because you are so funny!"

Later, the lion was having a drink at a stream. He saw that a campfire blazed across the way. The camp was empty.

tangled:

"Hunters must be near," he said. Just then a net fell on him. The lion was **tangled** in it. He roared with all his might.

④ Reread Reread page 112. What details tell you that the lion does not think a little mouse could help him? Write it below.

_____

_____

⑤ Read Underline the sentences that tell how the mouse helps the lion.

Suddenly, the mouse appeared. "I will get you out in no time."

The swift mouse **nibbled** at the net. Soon, the lion was free.

"I didn't believe you could help me," said the lion. "You saved my life."

"It was simply my turn to help you," said the mouse.

nibbled:

SHORT RESPONSE

Cite Text Evidence   Reread the story. What lesson does this story tell? Write the lesson below.

_____

_____

Background Soil is the top layer of Earth. Plants grow in soil. There are many different kinds of soil.

Setting a Purpose Read to find out the different kinds of soil and what soil is made of.

Super Soil

1 Read Underline the words that help you know what the word *humus* means.

Soil contains many things. When insects, leaves, and twigs die and break down in the soil, they become humus. Tiny bits of broken rock are also found in soil. Soil holds water and air, too. The amount of humus, rock, air, and water in soil **differs** from place to place.

differs:

2 Reread Reread page 115. Would you find the same amount of humus in all types of soil? How do you know? Write it below.

_____

_____

③ Read Underline a sentence that tells about the best kind of soil for growing crops.

fortunate:

If someone promised to give you good soil for growing crops, what kind of soil would you be **fortunate** enough to get? Soil with lots of humus is best for growing crops.

All plants need water. They take water in through roots that grow underneath the ground. They need just the right amount of water for sprouting new growth. Too little water is harmful to plants and may cause drooping leaves.

Corn is an important crop in the United States. To grow, it needs soil with lots of humus.

④ Reread Reread page 116. How do plants get the water they need? Write it below.

_____

_____

⑤ Read Underline the sentence that tells about plants that can store water.

Deserts are places that get little rain. There is not much humus in desert soil either. Most desert plants have **shallow** roots. The roots spread out just below the ground to catch rain water. Cactus plants store water in their stems.

shallow:

SHORT RESPONSE

Cite Text Evidence   How do desert plants get water? Write it below.

_____

_____

_____

6 **Read** Underline the text that tells why the creosote bush grows well in dry desert soil.

A creosote bush has waxy leaves that do not lose water in the hot sun. These plants grow well in dry desert soil. Many cactus plants have beautiful flowers. After the flowers have **blossomed**, they produce many tiny seeds.

blossomed:

7 **Reread** Reread page 118. What happens after cactus flowers have blossomed? Write it below.

_____

_____

⑧ Read Circle the information in the chart that describes sandy soil.

Kinds of Soil

Topsoil	Clay Soil	Sandy Soil
• has a lot of humus • is dark in color • is best for plant growth	• is made of tiny clay pieces • is sticky when wet • is brown, red, or yellow	• has a lot of weathered rock • feels gritty • is tan or light brown

SHORT RESPONSE

(*Cite Text Evidence*)   Reread pages 115–119. What type of soil in the chart would be best for growing crops? Write one reason from the text that tells why.

_____

_____

UNIT 6
What a Surprise!

Background A life cycle is the different parts of a living thing's life. A life cycle goes from the time an animal is born to the time it is an adult.

Setting a Purpose Read to learn about the life cycle of a frog.

From Eggs to Frogs

①Read Underline the sentence that tells what a tadpole looks like.

From Egg to Tadpole

Many frogs start life as an egg that hatches in an ordinary pond. The young are called tadpoles. You may look at them suspiciously and feel confused. Why? Tadpoles look like tiny fish, not frogs.

② **Read** Underline a sentence that tells where a tadpole lives and how it breathes.

From Tadpole to Frog

A tadpole has a tail but no legs. It uses its tail to stay in control as it swims. A tadpole lives underwater and breathes through **gills**. As a tadpole grows, it begins to look like a frog. A frog has legs and lungs but no tail. A frog lives out of water part of the time.

gills:

a tadpole swimming

③ **Reread** Reread page 123. Find out two ways that a frog is different from a tadpole. Write them below.

_____

_____

_____

④ Read Circle the part of the diagram that shows how a frog's life starts.

① A frog lays lots of eggs.

② Tadpoles hatch from the eggs.

③ The tadpole grows legs. Lungs develop. The tail shrinks.

④ The tadpole has become a frog.

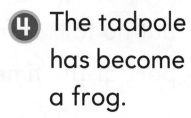

⑤ Reread Reread the diagram. What part of the frog's life cycle comes after a tadpole hatches?

_____

_____

⑥ Read Circle the heading on this page.

Some animals care for their young and teach them how to find food. A tadpole gets no training from its parents. It is able to find its own food.

Frogs as Pets

It is a good idea to keep your frog in a fish tank, not a cage. Put water in the tank and rocks for the frog to climb on. **Sensible** owners handle their frogs gently so the frogs do not become upset. They give their frogs water, plants, and the good food they need.

sensible:

SHORT RESPONSE

(*Cite Text Evidence*) Reread pages 122–125. How does the diagram of the life cycle of a frog help you understand the text? Write it below.

_____

_____

Background A fossil is what is left of a plant or an animal that lived long ago. Some fossils are found in tar. Tar is a black, sticky material that is found in the ground in some places.

Setting a Purpose Read to find out how animals long ago became fossils in a tar pit in Los Angeles.

La Brea Tar Pits

by Ciara McLaughlin

CLOSE READ
Notes

① **Read** Underline what scientists find in the tar pits.

pits:

Did you know that Los Angeles, California, is famous for its tar **pits**? They are the La Brea Tar Pits, to be exact. Scientists remove lots of fossils from them. Many people are amazed to see the fossils.

② **Read** Underline a sentence that tells how scientists know that Los Angeles was once cooler and wetter.

Scientists have explained that Los Angeles was once cooler and wetter than it is today. They know this because fossils of plants and animals that lived only in cool, wet places have been discovered there. These plants and animals lived a very long time ago. The animals included big cats with huge teeth. Imagine how they growled! Other animals had to be **on guard** if they did not want to be eaten.

on guard:

Scientists search for fossils at the La Brea Tar Pits.

③ **Reread** Reread page 127. What is one kind of animal that got trapped in the tar pits? Write it below.

_____

_____

④ Read Underline the names of two other animals that were trapped in the tar pits.

mammoths:

At times, wolves chased **mammoths** into tar pits. Then the sticky tar trapped them all. The trapped animals died. Over time, they became fossils. The tar still traps living things. In time, they may become fossils. People may find them and keep them as souvenirs.

Life-size statues of mammoths at the La Brea Tar Pits.

⑤ Reread Reread page 128. How were mammoths trapped in the tar pits? Write it below.

_____

_____

6 Read In the time line, circle the event that happened about 40,000 years ago.

La Brea Time Line

More than 100,000 years ago	About 100,000 years ago	About 40,000 years ago	Today
Area covered by water	Water goes down, and land appears	First plants and animals trapped	Surrounded by a busy city

A saber-toothed cat skull

SHORT RESPONSE

Cite Text Evidence   Reread the time line. In your own words, tell the events that happened at La Brea from first to last. Write them below.

_____

_____

_____

_____

Background Cinderella has to get used to a new mother and two new sisters. Her new family members are not very nice to her.

Setting a Purpose Read to find out what happens when Cinderella makes a special wish.

Cinderella

by Sheila Sweeny Higginson
illustrated by Donald Wu

① Read Underline the start of the story that shows it is a fairy tale.

Once upon a time, there lived a girl named Cinderella. Cinderella was smart, kind, and beautiful. Her father loved her very much, and she loved him.

Cinderella had a stepmother and two stepsisters, too. They did not love Cinderella. They were jealous of her and were never kind.

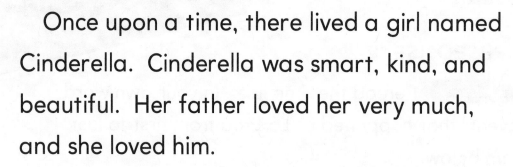

130

② **Read** Underline the details that show that Cinderella had to work hard.

Cinderella had to do all of the chores. She mopped the floors and washed all of the dirty dishes. She dusted, scrubbed, and polished every single thing in the house.

One day, Cinderella's family received an invitation to a **ball**. The prince was having a dance and inviting all of the young women in the kingdom.

ball:

③ **Reread** Reread pages 130–131. What details let you know that Cinderella's stepmother and stepsisters do not love her? Write them below.

_____

_____

④ **Read** In the picture, circle the fairy godmother's wand.

wand:

Cinderella ironed her stepsisters' dresses. She brushed their hair and fixed their bows. Then she waved good-bye as they skipped off to the ball. Cinderella was not allowed to go. After everyone left the house, Cinderella sat alone by the fireplace and cried. Tears streamed down her beautiful face. "Oh, how I wish that I could go to the ball," Cinderella sobbed. "I wish that I had a beautiful dress to wear."

Just then, a tiny woman with wings flew through the window. She had a **wand** in her hand. It was Cinderella's fairy godmother!

⑤ **Reread** Reread page 132. Underline the two things that Cinderella wishes for.

6 Read Underline three things that could only happen in a fairy tale.

"Why are you crying, my dear?" the fairy godmother asked Cinderella.

"I want to go to the ball, too," cried Cinderella.

"Then you shall go!" said the fairy godmother.

Cinderella's fairy godmother waved her wand quickly in the air. Poof! A pumpkin **transformed** into a golden coach. Six mice turned into a team of horses to pull the coach. Whoosh! Cinderella's old, worn-out clothes were changed into a beautiful pink and silver gown and two glass slippers.

transformed:

SHORT RESPONSE

Cite Text Evidence   Reread pages 130–133. How does Cinderella's fairy godmother make Cinderella's wishes come true? Write it below.

_____

_____

⑦ Read In the picture, circle the coach that takes Cinderella to the ball.

"What are you waiting for?" the fairy godmother asked Cinderella. "You need to get to the ball! Just make sure that you come home by midnight."

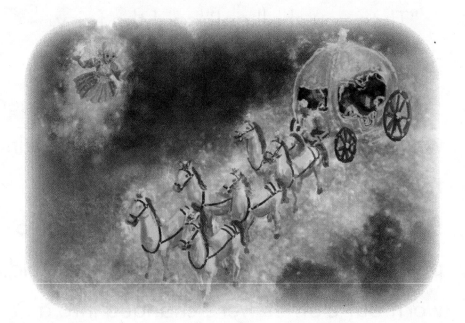

The prince saw Cinderella as soon as she entered the ballroom. He could not believe his eyes. She was the most beautiful girl he had ever seen.

⑧ Reread Reread page 134. What does Cinderella have to remember to do by midnight? Write it below.

_____

9 **Read** Underline four words that describe Cinderella and the prince.

The prince asked Cinderella to dance. The prince soon discovered that Cinderella was smart and kind, and he fell completely in love with her. Cinderella learned that the prince was good and **noble**. Cinderella fell in love with him, too.

noble:

SHORT RESPONSE

Cite Text Evidence Reread pages 134–135. Why do Cinderella and the prince fall in love with each other? Write it below.

_____

_____

⑩ Read In the picture, circle the glass slipper that falls off Cinderella's foot.

Soon enough, the clock began to strike midnight in the ballroom. Cinderella gasped and turned to race out of the castle. As she ran out, one of her glass slippers fell off her foot. Cinderella did not stop to get it.

⑪ Reread Reread page 136. What clue does Cinderella leave that might help the prince find her? Use details from the text to write the answer below.

_____

_____

12 Read Underline a sentence that tells what the prince vows to do.

The prince rushed after Cinderella, but he couldn't catch her. He picked up the glass slipper and sighed. It belonged on the foot of the girl he loved. He **vowed** to find Cinderella and marry her.

The prince was true to his word. With the glass slipper in hand, he knocked on every door in the kingdom. He was looking for the girl whose foot would fit into the slipper.

vowed:

13 Reread Reread page 137. What was the prince's plan to find Cinderella? Use details from the text to write the answer.

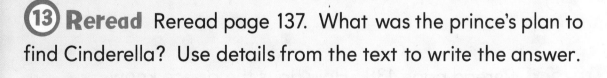

14 Read Underline the sentences that show that the stepsisters want the glass slipper to fit them.

Every girl wished the slipper would fit, especially Cinderella's stepsisters. The stepsisters tugged and pulled on the slipper. They pushed with all their might, but they could not fit their big feet into the slipper.

Cinderella watched her stepsisters as she stood next to the fireplace. At last, she stepped out so that the prince could see her.

"May I try?" she asked shyly.

The prince knelt down in front of Cinderella and held out the glass slipper. Cinderella placed her foot into the slipper, and it fit her **perfectly**.

perfectly:

15 Reread Reread page 138. How does the prince know he has found the girl he fell in love with? Write it below.

_____

_____

138

16 **Read** Underline a sentence that tells how everything turns out in the end.

However, the prince did not need to see that. He looked into Cinderella's eyes. He knew that she was his true love.

The prince took Cinderella back to his castle, and they were married the next day. Then Cinderella, who was always kind, invited her father, her stepmother, and her stepsisters to live with the prince and her in the castle. They all lived happily ever after.

SHORT RESPONSE

Cite Text Evidence What lesson does this story tell? Write the lesson below.

_____

_____

Background Sometimes people act shy around new people. But often they find out that strangers can be nice.

Setting a Purpose Read to find out how a stranger makes soup with a stone.

Readers' Theater

Stone Soup

adapted by Greta McLaughlin

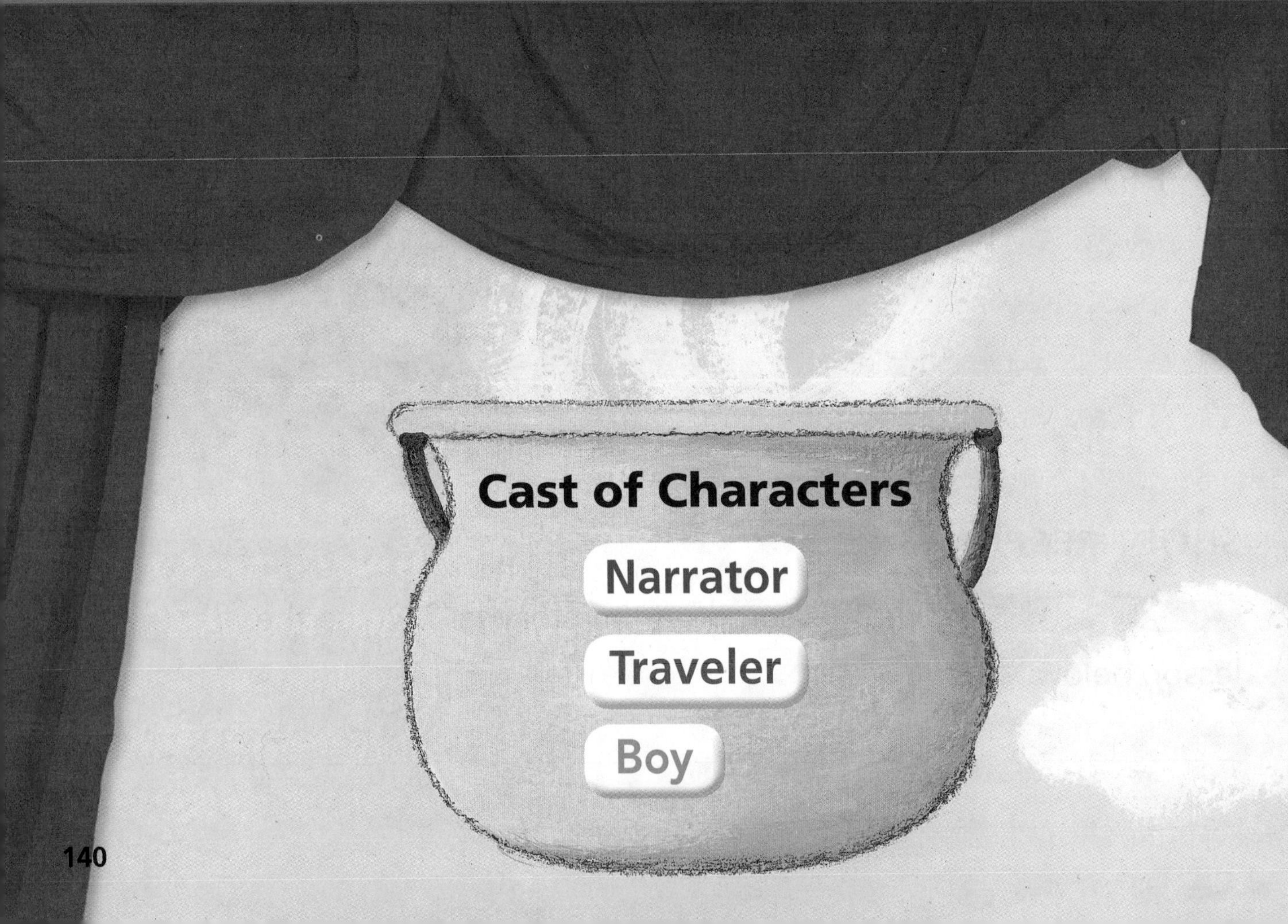

Cast of Characters
Narrator
Traveler
Boy

1 Read Underline the sentence that shows what the traveler wants from the villagers.

Narrator: A hungry man set out to search for food. He stopped in a village and knocked on the door of every home.

Traveler: Please, could you share some food with me?

Narrator: It **startled** the villagers to see a stranger. They would not share with him. The man leaned against a well. He took a pot out of his sack and filled it with water.

startled:

Boy: What are you doing?

2 Reread Reread page 141. Why do the villagers not share with the traveler? Write it below.

_____

_____

③ Read Underline the sentence that tells what the traveler is making.

Traveler: I've tossed a stone into my pot so I can make stone soup.

Boy: That's odd. Is stone soup good?

Traveler: It is. But the soup would be better if I had a carrot.

Boy: Grandma grows carrots. I'll ask her for one.

Traveler: Thank you. Please, ask her to join us for soup.

④ Reread Reread page 142. What does the traveler do to get food for the soup? Write it below.

_____

_____

⑤ Read Underline the foods that the villagers give to the boy.

Narrator: The boy stopped at all the villagers' homes. He **gathered** food to put into the pot. Soon the soup contained carrots, green beans, potatoes, and more.

gathered:

Boy: Is the soup ready?

Traveler: Yes, it is just right.

Narrator: The man shared his soup with the grateful villagers. In turn, they made sure that he never went hungry again.

SHORT RESPONSE

Cite Text Evidence   Reread pages 141–143. What lesson does this traditional tale teach about life? How do you know? Write it below

_____

_____

Background A model citizen is someone who other people admire and look up to. A model citizen is a good example for other people.

Setting a Purpose Read to find out why Benjamin Franklin was a model citizen.

A Model Citizen

① Read Underline three reasons why Ben Franklin became famous.

Ben Franklin became famous for many reasons. He spent large amounts of his time doing scientific experiments. He designed new inventions. He owned a newspaper and composed many stories for it.

② **Read** Underline two reasons why Ben Franklin was a good citizen.

Franklin was a good citizen. He began the first fire company in America. He also started the first public library. As a result, life was better for people.

In 1776, Great Britain had **colonies** in America. People in the colonies wanted to be free. They fought the Revolutionary War against Britain to become free.

colonies:

③ **Reread** Reread page 145. Why did people in the colonies fight the Revolutionary War? Write it below.

_____

_____

④ **Read** Underline the name of the new country that Ben Franklin helped.

achieve:

The colonists asked Franklin to help them **achieve** freedom. He helped Thomas Jefferson write the Declaration of Independence. The thirteen colonies won the war in 1783 and became the United States of America.

⑤ **Reread** Reread page 146. What is something Ben Franklin did to help the colonists achieve freedom? Write it below.

_____

_____

_____

6 Read On the map, circle the colony of Pennsylvania.

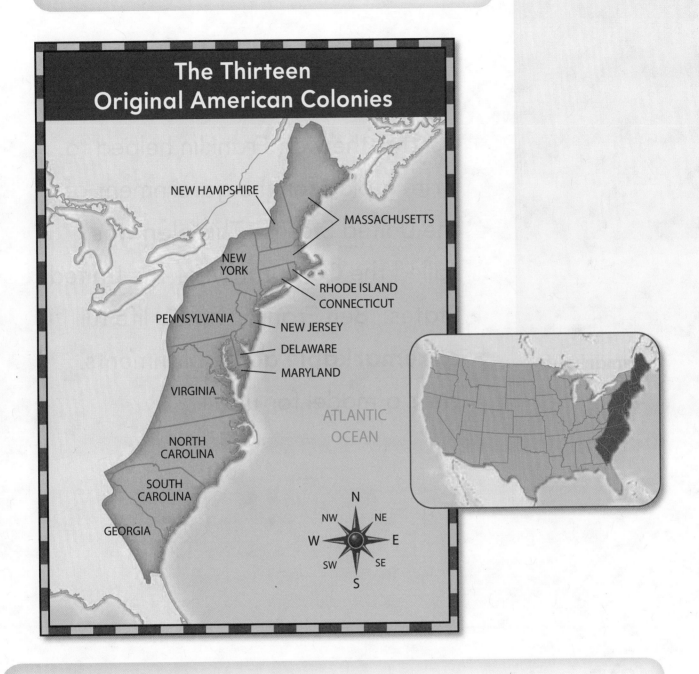

The Thirteen Original American Colonies

NEW HAMPSHIRE

MASSACHUSETTS

NEW YORK

RHODE ISLAND
CONNECTICUT

PENNSYLVANIA

NEW JERSEY

DELAWARE

MARYLAND

VIRGINIA

ATLANTIC
OCEAN

NORTH CAROLINA

SOUTH CAROLINA

GEORGIA

N
NW   NE
W   E
SW   SE
S

SHORT RESPONSE

Cite Text Evidence   Reread page 147. What does the map show you about where the thirteen colonies were? Write it below.

_____

_____

7 Read Underline the name of the new plan for the government of the United States.

After the war, Franklin helped to write a plan for the government of the United States. This plan was called the Constitution of the United States. Ben Franklin had a life full of **remarkable** accomplishments. He is a model for us all.

remarkable:

8 Reread Reread page 148. How did Ben Franklin help the government of his new country? Write it below.

_____

_____

_____

9 Read Compare the picture of Ben Franklin on page 145 with the painting here. Read the caption on this page. Then circle Ben Franklin in this painting.

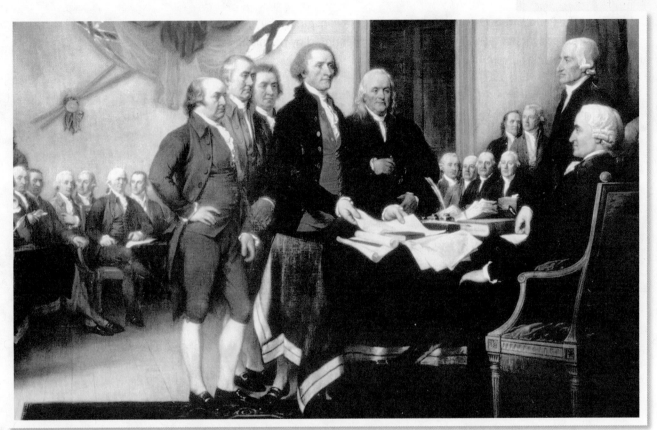

This painting shows the signing of the Declaration of Independence. Franklin is standing beside Thomas Jefferson.

SHORT RESPONSE

Cite Text Evidence   What are two reasons why Ben Franklin was a model for us all? Write them below.

_____

_____

_____

Acknowledgments

"Grandpa's Stories" from *The Collected Poems of Langston Hughes* by Langston Hughes, edited by Arnold Rampersad with David Roessel, Associate Editor. Text copyright © 1994 by The Estate of Langston Hughes. Reprinted by permission of Alfred A. Knopf, an imprint of Knopf Doubleday Publishing Group, a division of Random House LLC, and Harold Ober Associates Incorporated. Any third party use of this material, outside of this publication, is prohibited. Interested parties must apply directly to Random House LLC for permission. All rights reserved.

"The Period" from *On Your Marks: A Package of Punctuation* by Richard Armour. Text copyright © 1969 by Richard Armour. Reprinted by permission of Geoffrey Armour.

"Weather" from *Catch a Little Rhyme* by Eve Merriam. Text copyright © 1966, renewed © 1994 by Eve Merriam. Reprinted by permission of Marian Reiner. All rights reserved.